An Essential Guide for the ENFJ Personality Type

Insight into ENFJ Personality Traits and Guidance for Your Career and Relationships (MBTI ENFJ)

by Meghan Boone

Table of Contents

Introduction

Wouldn't it be great to know what life decisions are best for you based on your personality type? Luckily, the Myers-Briggs Type Indicator allows people to know just that. Having knowledge of the sixteen personality types in the MBTI can give us an understanding of people's distinct personality traits. This information can be used to determine the right jobs and the suitable romantic partners for everyone.

Among the sixteen personality types in the Myers-Briggs Type Indicator is the ENFJ, which stands for Extravert, Intuitive, Feeling, and Judging. This is probably one of the best personality types out there, so if it's yours, then rejoice! But what exactly makes the ENFJ different from the rest? First of all, they are natural-born leaders; second, they are altruistic; and third, they are idealistic. The ENFJ are good people and they also believe that others are equally good. They dream of a perfect world and they strive to make everything the way they think it should be. They are dependable and trustworthy, making them excellent friends and workmates. As leaders, the ENFJs uphold what's right and they always find the most peaceful way to solve conflicts. Having powerful intuitive abilities, the ENFJ can create meaningful connections with those around him. He is friendly, sociable, perceptive, and he knows all the right things to say.

Very few personality types are as fascinating and likeable as the ENFJ. People are naturally drawn to them due to their generosity, sincerity, and ability to communicate effectively. With such positive personality traits, the ENFJ can make the best leaders if given the right opportunity. But will that make them good lovers too? Who's your perfect romantic partner? Will your personality traits also work well in the position of a subordinate? What kinds of jobs will give fulfillment to the ENFJ? One by one, your questions will be answered. Read this book and find out what kind of lover, coworker, friend, and parent the ENFJ can be. Moreover, get to know yourself as an ENFJ and understand what drives you to succeed in love, your career, and in life.

Chapter 1: Understanding the ENFJ Personality Type

What do U.S. presidents Abraham Lincoln, Ronald Reagan, and Barack Obama have in common? All of them have the ENFJ Personality Type. ENFJ or Extravert, Intuitive, Feeling, Judging is one of the sixteen personality types in the Myers-Briggs Type Indicator. Individuals that belong to this group possess magnetism that naturally draws people to them. They make good leaders because they are able to inspire and influence others to act and make a difference in the world. Furthermore, they are confident and have the ability to guide people towards development and progress. Due to the distinct personality traits of the ENFJ, many of them are fit to become educators, trainers, and political leaders.

The ENFJ may be few, but they are popular and well-liked. Individuals that have this personality type possess an innate desire to help, and those that are familiar with them know that their concern for others is genuine. ENFJ individuals are often described as confident, assertive, and brave. They stand up for what's right and they are never afraid to speak their minds especially on topics that they deem important. Because of their strong intuitive ability, they find it easy to emotionally, spiritually, and mentally connect with someone they've just met. They are able to approach new people, make friends easily, and they have the power to create meaningful conversations. Their intuition also allows them to accurately read between the lines and understand the motivations behind people's actions. With this knowledge, the ENFJ are able to effectively give their assistance to those that are in need.

While some will have a hard time in trusting other people, the ENFJ are able to easily place their trust in individuals who they believe in. When they really have faith in someone, they will spend a lot of their time and effort trying to help this person out. They can dedicate their full attention to the issues that matter to them and they will always be willing to go out of their way just to support a cause that they believe in. Through the selfless behavior of the ENFJ, those that they have aided and those that witness their wholehearted actions strive to emulate their example. They inspire others to also do good and become more productive members of the society.

There are no better leaders than the ENFJ. They are sincere, compassionate, kindhearted individuals who are always willing to lend a helping hand. They can sacrifice their personal time in order to promote development and improvement. The ENFJ are happiest when they are given opportunities to take charge. They are eager to take on their duties and they can even go beyond what is expected of them when it comes to being a leader. But the best thing about having an ENFJ in charge is that he inspires his followers to reach higher, and to do better. He possesses the kind of enthusiasm that is totally infectious. His charisma is proven to unite people towards a common goal. They say that real altruism does not exist but in the case of ENFJs, you see a person that really wants to help without any ulterior motive. If you ask me, that's the quality of a natural-born leader.

Chapter 2: The Strengths and Weaknesses of an ENFJ

One of the best ways to understand the ENFJ personality type is by enumerating its strengths and weaknesses. People are usually known by their good and bad traits. But in the case of the ENFJ, most of his strengths are also considered his weaknesses. Truly, the ENFJ is one of a kind. Here are some of the most common traits of the ENFJ.

ENFJ Strengths

Humble

ENFJs make good leaders because they have the ability to admit that they don't know everything. They are able to acknowledge other members of the team and listen to their opinions. He does not think that he is the best in the group and he does not believe that only he has good ideas. More than often, ENFJ leaders were not placed in their position due to their ambition to have authority, but instead, they were selected by people who are aware of their good heart and capability to lead.

Dependable

One can always count on the ENFJ to come through. These individuals never leave people hanging and they do their best to make sure that they don't let down those that are depending on them. This quality makes the ENFJ good leaders because they never abandon their responsibilities.

Inspiring

When the ENFJs speak to a crowd, they captivate their listeners with their natural charm and their ability to effectively communicate. They have a gift when it comes to choosing the best words to reach out to their listeners and to send a message. Thus, they are able to inspire people to act and to move forward.

Kindhearted

The ENFJs have a compassionate heart and their desire to help others is genuine. Once they hold positions of power, they are given more opportunities to do good deeds for the benefit of many. Their kindness is often infectious and those that see their authenticity are often influenced to do the same.

ENFJ Weaknesses

Too Trusting

Due to their good nature, ENFJs believe that all people are good. And although individuals with the ENFJ personality have a strong intuition when it comes to people's feelings and motives, they might not correctly discern any shady intentions that some folks may have. They can become too trusting especially when they believe in the person.

Self-Sacrificing

The ENFJs are known to be compassionate and kindhearted. However, they can become too generous with their time, energy, and resources that some individuals can see it as an opportunity to benefit themselves. Furthermore, they can become too absorbed in other folk's issues that they are left spent and unable to continue helping others.

Decision-Making Issues

The ENFJs care deeply about the welfare of those around them. If at all possible, the ENFJ leader would not want anyone to be at the bad end of a decision that they have to make. As a result, he may have a hard time coming up with final decisions.

Unstable Self-Esteem

The ENFJs are capable leaders who have a kind heart. One might think that those qualities should be enough to give one a stable and overflowing self-confidence, but that's not the case with the ENFJs. Their self-esteem can fluctuate depending on their ability to meet their own expectations of themselves. They are always conscious about whether they already did their best or they could have done much better.

Too Much Empathy

Individuals that have the ENFJ personality trait are very sensitive to other people's feelings and emotions. They may try to get involved in issues that do not concern them or can do nothing about. As a result, the ENFJs can become too preoccupied about the conditions of those around them.

Chapter 3: The ENFJ as a Friend, Romantic Partner, and Parent

Individuals that belong to the ENFJ personality type are peaceful, loyal, and generous to a fault. To become friends with an ENFJ is never difficult as they are sociable, likable, and they truly enjoy getting to know others. When it comes to relationships, whether in friendship or in romance, the ENFJ always tries to create long-lasting alliances. They don't like insincere interactions and would only invest in connections that can result to meaningful relationships. As parents, the ENFJ are loving, supportive, and encouraging to their children. Kids of the ENFJ are lucky to have parents that are genuinely good people.

Friendship

Individuals that have the ENFJ personality trait work to maintain meaningful connections with their friends. Once they meet a kindred spirit, they will never let this person just drift away. The ENFJ are the kind of people that still have contact with friends from elementary, summer camp, high school, and college. Perhaps this can be attributed to the ENFJ's desire for genuine relations with people. The ENFJ can talk to anyone and they have no reservations about striking conversations with people they've just met. Due to their sincerity, people often accept the ENFJs easily and respond to them warmly and positively.

Everyone wants a friend that they can rely on, and that is what the ENFJ friend is all about. He is not a person that wastes time on superficial connections, but instead he is the type of individual that aims for real friendships. He is trustworthy and responsible. ENFJ friends have a positive outlook on life and they will often shine their brightness on the lives of those that are lucky enough to be in their circle. What makes the ENFJ a good pal is his genuine concern for those he regards as friends.

ENFJ friends can always be depended on to lend a helping hand. They will go out of their way to provide any assistance that their friends may need. They genuinely want their friends to be happy and successful. But again, some people will see this as an opportunity to take more from the friendship. ENFJ friends are selfless and idealistic so they will never suspect or accept that a friend might already be abusing their friendship.

Romance

The ENFJs love to be in a relationship. They enjoy the company of someone they deeply care about. People that belong in this group are looking for long-term relationships and they are not the type to play around. Once they've decided to pursue a romantic relationship, they will put all of their effort into making the bond strong and lasting. For those that have a romantic link with an ENFJ, you won't need to worry about the direction that your relationship is going. Because for the ENFJ, being in a relationship is a serious commitment and not just some pastime.

During the course of a romantic relationship, the ENFJ will not waste time in proving to his special someone that he is a worthy partner. Anyone who's in a relationship with an ENFJ will know firsthand how dependable this person can be. He keeps his word and he honors his obligations. While many grumble that their partners are insensitive to their needs, the lover of the ENFJ will never have this grievance. People that belong to the ENFJ group are perceptive and they have a knack for reading into their partner's behavior. As a result, they are almost always able to meet their lover's physical and emotional needs.

The ENFJ possesses a lot of good traits for a partner such as kindness, sensitivity, and dependability. Many will feel lucky to be in a relationship with people from this personality type. Nevertheless, one should keep in mind that the strengths of the ENFJ can also become his weaknesses. He can become overly sensitive to his partner's needs, so that he might come across as being clingy or needy. Since individuals that have this personality are selfless by nature, they would be willing to sacrifice their own happiness just to see their loved one satisfied. Most people with this personality trait despise confrontations, aggression, and violence of any kind. They are very good communicators so they will strive to resolve any misunderstanding through effective communication. All too often, they would put aside their own principles just to avoid any conflict with their partner. ENFJ lovers are known to be dependable and they thrive in the stability of routines. For those that like spontaneity in their romantic life, the ENFJ may not be a very good choice for a partner.

Parenthood

ENFJ parents are good role models for their children. Through their consistent examples, their kids can easily learn about kindness, compassion, and sincerity. Kids of the ENFJ are able to witness giving help without asking for something in return. Parents that belong to the ENFJ group can teach their young ones how to be a good leader. And even when they don't directly teach their kids about these good values, the children are able to see this and learn it through the examples given by their parents.

ENFJ parents are very good communicators and their intuitive nature allows them to understand their children better. As a result, they are able to communicate with their children about their issues. They also rely on effective communication when teaching discipline to their child. ENFJ parents don't see the point of harsh disciplinary methods because they know that words should be enough to reach out to their children. Due to the positive environment provided by ENFJ parents, their kids will naturally adopt values such as kindness, sincerity, humility, and leadership.

Chapter 4: Choosing the Best Career for an ENFJ

As mentioned earlier, the ENFJs are altruistic and they feel happiest when they are able to aid someone in any way that they are able to. They thrive in careers where they can share their knowledge, motivate people, and lead them towards improvement. Due to the unselfish qualities of the people that belong to the ENFJ group, they will always look for work that gives them opportunities to help. They consider a job meaningful work when they are able to connect with others and reach out to them.

ENFJs can make the most dedicated and the most effective educators. Teaching is a profession that requires patience, kindness, humility, and the genuine desire to teach/help. The ENFJs make the best teachers because they possess all of these traits. A person who has ENFJ personality traits will find the teaching profession very fulfilling.

Although the ENFJs are not overly ambitious when it comes to gaining power and authority, they can make effective political leaders. The genuine concern for people and their betterment is what drives the ENFJ politician to make a difference. Unfortunately, the ENFJ group is very small and not all who are in positions of power have the admirable qualities of an ENFJ leader.

Religious work can also prove very fulfilling for people with the ENFJ personality trait. It allows them to engage in activities where they can be in contact with people that really need help. Social work is also very appealing to this group of individuals because they have a real concern for those in dire conditions.

We can't help reiterating the fact that ENFJ individuals are very perceptive, since it is a characteristic that affects every aspect of their dealings with others. Their intuition allows them to read into people's motives and they are able to understand behaviors. They are also very sensitive to other people's feelings and emotions. A career in Human Resources can be a good match for the ENFJ. They also make excellent managers due to their people skills and good communication style.

ENFJs can also make great salespeople. They possess a natural charisma that attracts people to them. Customers can listen for hours to an ENFJ salesman. Don't forget the ENFJs ability to use words to influence others. They could start a career in advertising or be a marketing executive. Individuals who belong to this personality group have the power to inspire. Therefore, they can make excellent public and motivational speakers, too.

The jobs that don't match with the ENFJ personality are those that limit his ability to interact with people, inspire others, share his experiences, and hinder him from helping out with anything. They can also do badly in jobs that require them to make cutthroat decisions that could negatively affect the lives of other employees. For instance, they could make good hiring officers but they would be bad at firing or giving disciplinary actions to subordinates.

The best jobs for people that belong to the ENFJ group are those that require people skills and communication skills. In general, the ENFJ are responsible employees that always perform their duties well. They are considered assets in the workforce, whatever the job might be.

Chapter 5: The ENFJ's Workplace Behavior and Ethics

The ENFJ are popular in the workplace because of they are friendly, warm, and sincere people. No matter what job position they hold, they are able to work well with their colleagues and thrive in their roles in the company. With the positive qualities of the ENFJs, career success is always within reach.

People that belong to the ENFJ personality group have a fluctuating self-esteem. They are often insecure about the quality of their work and they always wonder if their efforts are satisfactory or not. They are constantly reviewing their work and they are never hesitant to ask people around them for feedback. They value criticisms and always look at it as a tool necessary for improvement. This attitude of the ENFJ worker allows him to offer high quality job performance that eventually benefits the company.

It's great to have ENFJ individuals in the team because they are diligent workers. They are responsible and they could always be counted upon to deliver what is expected of them. It is also not uncommon for ENFJ employees to give more than what their job requires of them. Keep in mind that the ENFJ are altruistic and they are always willing to help even if that entails doing additional work. They are also not interested in getting compensation for their extra work as long as they believe that they are helping others. People that have the ENFJ personality type always volunteer for tasks that nobody wants to take. He will do this because he sincerely wants to help and in order to keep the peace. Unfortunately, those they work for and work with may take advantage of the kindheartedness of the ENFJ. As a result, the ENFJ can become overworked and may not find real happiness in his workplace. For instance, a boss can give too much work to the ENFJ, because he is always willing to do it. It doesn't help that the ENFJ has an unstable self-confidence, as this causes him not to want to disappoint by refusing additional tasks even when he is already overworked.

Individuals that have the ENFJ personality type dislike confrontations and conflicts. They will always strive to maintain peace in the workplace by getting along as best as they can with their colleagues and superiors. They are cooperative and they are good followers as well as leaders. ENFJs are perceptive—yes, we keep emphasizing this quality because it's remarkable—and they use this gift in order to create harmonious working relationships with all people in the workplace. As colleagues, they are not competitive but instead they will go out of their way to help a flailing coworker to do better at his job. They sincerely want people to be successful at what they do.

Unlike the other personality types, the ENFJ can do well as a subordinate or as a boss. They are good subordinates, coworkers, and they are even better superiors. There is a reason why people that belong to this personality group should have positions of power, though. Remember that the ENFJs are altruistic. They have an innate desire to help others. Just imagine the good that they can do when they are given opportunities to share their knowledge and to connect with more people.

As managers, ENFJ individuals are the best. They have real concern for their subordinates' needs as employees and as people. Many people that sit in management positions have lost their ability to relate with those in the lower part of the corporate pyramid. However, the ENFJ has empathy and he will never disregard his subordinates. He can relate to all types of people due to his friendly and sincere nature. ENFJ managers can communicate with all their subordinates. He uses his intuition to understand their feelings and needs. He can effectively handle any kind of unrest in the office just by sitting down with his subordinates and talking to them. Furthermore, an ENFJ manager is able to effectively manipulate his coworkers so that they can move in the right direction.

The ENFJs in the workplace are considered strengths of the company. Whether they hold low positions or

29

high positions, they make productive workers. They are honest, hardworking people. Through their sincere words and actions, they have the ability to inspire those around them to dream bigger, work harder, and reach higher.

Conclusion

In today's modern setting, the ENFJ personality type sounds too good to be true. Idealistic and altruistic just seems impossible to find together. Nevertheless, two percent of the world's population has this personality type and although they are few, this number should be enough to make a real difference in the world.

Many ENFJs have found their real calling and they are out there doing what they do best—helping. However, some may not have found the right path or are still unsure about which track to take. Hopefully, after reading this book, an ENFJ out there might better understand what his personality type is really about and learn how much he can do with the abilities he possesses. Or if you know someone who you think might be an ENFJ, then you can help him make the right direction in his life.

Having an understanding of the ENFJ personality type helps us identify what careers are the best match for these individuals. For instance, we have determined that people with this personality type thrive best in management positions. But in general, they will be happy in jobs where they are able to help others.

By knowing the personality traits of the ENFJs, it would be easy to determine the perfect partner for them. Individuals from this group are very sensitive to the needs of their lovers. They are always asking their partner if they can do anything more for them. And while some will find this adorable, others may feel suffocated by all the attention. Knowing this helps those that are presently in a relationship with an ENFJ. They will understand that the ENFJs are not needy or clingy but just sincerely concerned for other people.

Awareness and familiarity of the sixteen personality types in the MBTI can help anyone in choosing the right career path as well as the perfect love match. After reading this book, we hope to have helped you understand the ENFJ personality trait better. May you use this knowledge in your journey to find happiness in your friendships, career, family life, and love life.

Finally, I'd like to thank you for purchasing this book! If you enjoyed it or found it helpful, I'd greatly appreciate it if you'd take a moment to leave a review on Amazon. Thank you!

72638835R00022

Made in the USA
Middletown, DE
07 May 2018